100 Cowboy Bible Verses
Simplified Cowboy Version

Kevin Weatherby

Copyright © 2017 Kevin Weatherby

All rights reserved.

ISBN-10: 1541348389
ISBN-13: 978-1541348387

DEDICATION

This book is dedicated to all the cowboys, punchers, and buckaroos that are out there living the dream and riding for the Lord.

ACKNOWLEDGMENT

The Simplified Cowboy Version is not a bible. It was never intended to be a bible, nor should it be thought of as such. The SCV is a bible paraphrase intended to merely catch a glimpse of the bible's deep wisdom, and most importantly, to see Jesus Christ, through the eyes of a working ranch cowboy.

We hope that this book will encourage the reading of the real Word of God.

-Kevin Weatherby

#100

By this all men
will know that
you ride for me, if
you take care and
love one another.

John 13:35

#99

We have a Cowboy on our side that stands before God and completely understands everything we go through. He has trod every trail and experienced every situation, but he never made a mistake or sinned.

Hebrews 4:15

#98

"My thinkin' is not your thinkin', neither are your trails my trails, or your methods my methods," says the Lord.

Isaiah 55:8

#97

Let the light of
your fire shine
before men so that
they can see the
great things you
do and praise the
Boss in heaven.

Matthew 5:16

#96

What an amazin' thing it is when families can get along together. This unity is like a brisket rub made together of individual spices in equal measures, when brought together, is holy and pleasin' to God.

Psalm 133:1-2

#95

Jesus said, "Love the Boss with everything you've got."

Matthew 22:37

#94

Whatever you do, ride with all your heart, riding for the Lord, and not for men.

Colossians 3:23

#93

Then Jesus walked up to 'em and said, "I've been made Boss over heaven's Green Pastures and all the ranches of this world."

Matthew 28:18

#92

Don't let the Code of God
slip loose from you or
your thoughts; think about
it when the sun comes up
and when the nightbird
sings, so that you can be
sure to do everything in it.
Then you will find green
pastures with tall grass
and your herd will
succeed.

Joshua 1:8

#91

He swapped our sins for his perfect goodness. And he was punished for these sins by bein' nailed to a tree. He did this so we could be free of sin and ride the right trail; you have been completely healed by the wounds that killed him.

1 Peter 2:24

#90

You will dole out
peace to the
cowboy who
trusts you and
keeps his
thoughts on you.

Isaiah 26:3

#89

There is only one name by which you can be saved and this name is the only cowboy that can ride in and rescue you from the fires of hell.

Acts 4:12

#88

The Boss didn't send his only Son to come down here and tell you all the things you do wrong. He sent him to save everyone from the fires that never go out.

John 3:17

#87

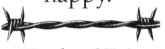

Be glad to ride for the Lord and he will make you happy.

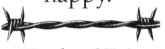

Psalm 37:4

#86

Ride right up to God with your head held high so you can receive his mercy and find the help you need.

Hebrews 4:16

#85

Just like rain
comes from above
to fall on thirsty
pastures, the Lord
will send blessings
and eternal life to
his cowboys and
cowgirls.

Psalm 133:3

#84

You can be sure that the Cowboy who started you on the right trail will ride with you until the end.

Philippians 1:6

#83

He has given his word that you can ride with him and be untied from the ropes and chains of lust that have held you prisoner.

2 Peter 1:4

#82

Don't forget, as some have the habit of doing, that it's important to sit around the campfire and share each other's company. Give encouragement and spur each other on to good deeds—more and more as you see the Day comin' fast.

Hebrews 10:25

#81

I'm plum certain that neither livin' nor dyin', neither the angels from heaven nor the boogers from brush, neither the right now's nor the will be's, nor any force,…

Romans 8:38

#80

…there ain't no fence, no gate, nor any mountain or problem, that will be able to keep us from the love of God that is found in his only Son.

Romans 8:39

#79

Because you need to understand that only by bein' tested will your faith grow and be made stronger. You can't learn to ride rank by straddlin' a stick horse.

James 1:3

#78

That cowboy who keeps on ridin', even when it's hard, will prove he's authentic and get the great things their Dad has planned.

James 1:12

#77

To all who have chosen to saddle up with him, to those who believed in who they ride for, he gave 'em the right to become his own kids.

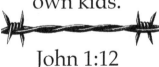

John 1:12

#76

Sure enough, faith comes from listenin' to the Good Story, and the Good Story is heard through the word of Christ.

Romans 10:17

#75

You have rode with the top cowboy, and he has showed you what is good. And what are our orders from the Boss? To act honorable, to love givin' folks a break, and to ride humbly with Him.

Micah 6:8

#74

There is no greater love than this: To take your place in the gunfight that you can't win.

John 15:13

#73

The word of God is alive and it rides far and wide. It's sharper than any castratin' knife, it penetrates even to seperatin' soul and spirit, rawhide and bone; it passes final judgement on the thinkin' and attitudes of a cowboy's way.

Hebrews 4:12

#72

I'm leavin' my peace with you. I'm not ever gonna come back and take it from you like the world does. With this here gift, there is never a need to worry or fret.

John 14:27

#71

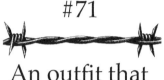

An outfit that gets along and works well together makes the Boss smile.

Psalm 133:1

#70

If you're ponderin' on what love really means, it's this: Jesus Christ swapped his life for ours and we should do the same for Him.

1 John 3:16

#69

Ain't nobody told you that the headquarters of God, where the Holy Spirit resides, doesn't lie on a hill, but in your heart? You get this spirit from God himself, so you don't ride for your own brand anymore, but for his.

1 Corinthians 6:19

#68

At the beginning of the trail was the Word, and the Word was with the Boss, and the Word was the Boss.

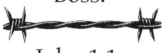

John 1:1

#67

And my God will fill your life and your pastures with everything you need accordin' to everything that was given to you through Jesus.

Philippians 4:19

#66

Now the Bereans
were better cowboys
than the
Thessalonians
because they listened
eagerly and went to
the Good Book to see
if what Paul was
talkin' about was
honest and true.

Acts 17:11

#65

So if you've done some things you ain't proud of, go to another cowboy and tell 'em about it and your heart will no longer be heavy. A fellow that rides hard and straight, his prayers are strong and they get the job done.

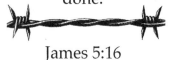

James 5:16

#64

Since there are so many cowboys and cowgirls around, let's cut the hobbles of sin that are keepin' us tied down. Let us ride with strength and power in the gatherin' that we've been called to.

Hebrews 12:1

#63

Since you've been
chosen by God to
ride for Him, clothe
yourselves with love
for one another, nice
words and deeds, not
thinking too mightily
of yourself, easy
going and patient.

Colossians 3:1

#62

So the Boss built cowboys to resemble Him and His nature; cowboy and cowgirl He created them.

Genesis 1:27

#61

My saddle won't
pinch and my
burden is lighter
than an empty
feed sack.

Matthew 11:30

#60

There ain't nothin'
that God can't do;
no matter what we
think we can ask
for or imagine. For
his glory, his spirit
is workin' inside
of us non-stop.

Ephesians 3:20

#59

Peter said, "Turn around and quit followin' the wrong trail. Be baptized, all of y'all, in the name of Jesus Christ and he will forgive your sorry ways, then you'll get the gift of the Holy Ghost."

Acts 2:38

#58

We've all thrown our heads up like wild cattle and run off to the brush to do what we wanted; and God has laid all of our punishment on His shoulders.

Isaiah 53:6

#57

Listen up cowboys, don't sweat it when you go through the rough and rank patches of life. Shoot, you ought to be glad you go through them because it's these things that'll sure enough make a man out of ya. These times will knock the quit right out of ya

James 1:2

#56

"Only those that hear what I have to say and believe in the one who sent me will enter the forever green pastures and escape the killer buyer. A cowboy who does this has rode from the jaws of death into the arms of life."

John 5:24

#55

You can't please the
Boss without havin'
faith, because in order
to knock on his door
you must believe that
he's there and he
surely gives favors to
those who know
where to look and who
can do it.

Hebrews 11:6

#54

Jesus told her, "I am life after death. Any cowboy or cowgirl that believes this will live even though their body will quit 'em."

John 11:25

#53

May the God of hope fill your tanks with water and your pastures with green grass as you trust in him. All you have will overflow with hope by the sheer might of the Holy Ghost.

Romans 15:13

#52

God had him, who had never done nothin' wrong, take our place in front of the firing squad so that because of him, we could be deemed worthy in God's eyes.

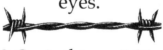

2 Corinthians 5:21

#51

He took all our wrongs and willingly took the punishment for us. And then we shunned him as if they were his problems instead of our own.

Isaiah 53:4

#50

For God didn't give us the spirit of a sissy, but a spirit of strength, love, and self-control.

2 Timothy 1:7

#49

You're gonna get a double shot of power when the Holy Ghost saddles up with you; and you're gonna tell my tale in cow camps all over the world.

Acts 1:8

#48

"I ain't said these things just to hear myself talk! I've said 'em so that you can have a better life with me. In this world you will have rank broncs and more trouble than you can handle, but don't get discouraged. I have whipped this old world."

John 16:33

#47

Ride with me and learn what I teach you, 'cause I'm a gentle trail boss and my heart is pure and humble. With me is where you'll find rest for your soul.

Matthew 11:29

#46

Then the Boss said, "Let Us make some folks in Our image, to be like Us. They'll be in charge of the fish, the birds, the livestock, all the wild critters on the earth, and the small critters that scamper along the ground."

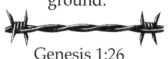

Genesis 1:26

#45

So don't be scared,
I'm right here; don't
be confused, for I am
your God. I will give
you the strength you
need and a helpin'
hand when you need
it. I'm gonna tie on
hard and fast to you.

Isaiah 41:10

#44

If you'll go ahead
and say out loud
that Jesus is Lord,
and believe with
all you got that his
Daddy brought
him back to life,
you will be saved.

Romans 10:9

#43

But he told me, "My grace is enough for you; I am strongest when you've been bucked off." Because of this, I will brag more about my weaknesses so his strength will rest upon me.

2 Corinthians 12:9

#42

Don't have a hankerin' for money. Be glad with what ya got, because the Big Boss has said, "I ain't never gonna leave ya, nor forsake ya."

Hebrews 13:5

#41

So if anyone is now ridin' for Christ, he is a brand spankin' new cowboy. The old fellow has been wadded up and thrown away like an old feed sack. He is like a blind man seein' his first sunrise.

2 Corinthians 5:17

#40

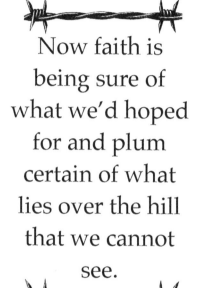

Now faith is being sure of what we'd hoped for and plum certain of what lies over the hill that we cannot see.

Hebrews 11:1

#39

Come and ride with
me, all of y'all that
are worn smooth out
and feel like a
miner's old pack
mule, and I will take
the load off of you
and let you lie down
in tall green grass.

Matthew 11:28

#38

That temptation that's got you hemmed up in the corner of the pen isn't anything that someone else hasn't fought before. And God is faithful; he won't let anything hook you that you cannot bear. But when you do face an ornery temptation that's on the fight, he will open the gate so you can escape.

1 Corinthians 10:13

#37

Like the greatest saddle maker ever, we were tooled by God himself, created in Christ Jesus to do good things that God prepared for us before we even got here.

Ephesians 2:10

#36

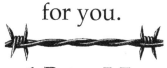

Pack up all your worryin' and stressin' and give it to Him… because he cares for you.

1 Peter 5:7

#35

Never take your eyes off of Jesus, the founder of our faith, who gave everything up and took himself to the cross, didn't care about the shame it caused him, and then hunkered down at God's right hand.

Hebrews 12:2

#34

Search first for his
outfit and his
way, and when
you find these,
you'll find the
rest of what you
need.

Matthew 6:33

#33

God wrote the Good Book by guidin' a man's hand. It is the perfect tool for attitude adjustin', training, learnin', and discoverin' the truth.

2 Timothy 3:16

#32

Make Jesus the boss
of your outfit.
Always be cinched
up tight and ready
to give someone the
hope that you have
found, but do so
with kind words
and a gentle spirit.

1 Peter 3:15

#31

But he was mauled
for our mistakes, he
was run-through for
our wrongs; he took
our place on the
gallows so that we
might have peace,
and by his pain we
are healed.

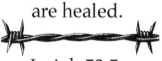

Isaiah 53:5

#30

…bein' gentle and keeping ourselves bridled and under control. God never said we couldn't do those things.

Galatians 5:23

#29

Sin's outfit pays in death, but God's gift is a trail into eternal life through Christ Jesus our Lord.

Romans 6:23

#28

No matter how tough you think you are, you can't save your own hide. You can't toot your own horn about something you can't do on your own.

Ephesians 2:9

#27

But those who hope in
the Lord will be able to
get back on. They will
ride to the top of
mountains; they will
thunder across the
plains, they will walk
courageous and stand
proud.

Isaiah 40:31

#26

Did I not tell you
what I wanted?
Be brave and
strong. Don't be a
sissy; do not lose
heart, for the Lord
your God will
always ride right
beside you.

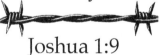

Joshua 1:9

#25

And the peace of God, which cannot be understood by our way of thinking, will guard your hearts and mind in Christ Jesus.

Philippians 4:7

#24

Finally, cowboys, whatever is sure 'nough true, whatever is just, whatever is no-nonsense, whatever is unpolluted, whatever is pretty as a newborn calf, whatever is worth admiring—if anything is worth its weight or deservin' of a smile—ponder on these things.

Philippians 4:8

#23

God proves that he
loves us because of
this: Even though
we were still loping
out in the pasture
and only living for
ourselves, Christ
died for us.

Romans 5:8

#22

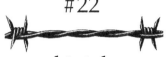

…teachin' them to ride the way I have taught y'all. And remember this, I am riding with you, even to the very end of every trail.

Matthew 28:20

#21

Jesus replied, "I am the trail that leads to forever. The only way to my Dad and heaven is to follow me."

John 14:6

#20

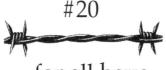

…for all have been bucked off and fallen short of the glory of God.

Romans 3:23

#19

If we spill the
beans about our
sins, he will do
what he says and
forgive us and
make us new.

1 John 1:9

#18

I have been placed in a pine box. I no longer live, but Christ is living in me. The life you see is one of riding in faith because he loves me and gave his life up for me.

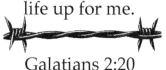

Galatians 2:20

#17

So Paul stayed with them until all the foals were comin' two year olds and taught the cowboys how to ride for the brand.

Acts 18:11

#16

One night the Lord spoke to Paul in a dream. "Don't be scared; keep on talkin' to them cowboys. Don't keep quiet."

Acts 18:9

#15

I'm ridin' with you and no one is gonna lay a finger on you. I've got cowboys everywhere.

Acts 18:10

#14

That old snake only comes to steal, murder, and change your brand; I have come to give you life, and give it abundantly.

John 10:10

#13

I'm saying this as if
the God of mercy
himself were
standing right here.
I urge each of you
to offer up your
lives into His outfit
—this is how you
really worship God.

Romans 12:1

#12

The offspring of the
Spirit is love, real
happiness, a
content heart, an
easy disposition,
sincere kindness,
perfect patience,
and bein' faithful.

Galatians 5:22

#11

It's our faith in
God's love for us
that does the saving
—and this is not
from our rope, or
our hand, or our
horse, it is the gift
of the Almighty.

Ephesians 2:8

#10

Ride out and gather cowboys and teach them to ride for me, dunk 'em in the name of the Father, the Son, and the Holy Ghost.

Matthew 28:19

#9

Don't stress about
nothing, but just
be thankful and
ask God for all
you need.

Philippians 4:6

#8

Quit tryin' to fit into
the sorry ways of the
world, but be made
new by changing the
way you think. Only
then will you find the
trail that the Boss
wants you to ride.

Romans 12:2

#7

Every step your horse takes is an opportunity to thank the Lord. God will blaze a straight trail for a thankful cowpuncher.

Proverbs 3:6

#6

Let the Lord have the reins of your life and pay no mind to what you know or don't know.

Proverbs 3:5

#5

Before any gate
was hung or any
wire was
stretched, God
made the heavens
and the earth.

Genesis 1:1

#4

Jesus is my strength, courage, and ability by which I can ride. With him I can cover any bronc and handle any situation.

Philippians 4:13

#3

We have no doubt that that all us cowboys and cowgirls that have answered his call, God will take the reins and lead us to green pastures.

Romans 8:28

#2

"I know the trail that I want you to ride," says the Lord, "this trail doesn't lead to a desert, but to green grass. In fact, it's the future that you prayed for."

Jeremiah 29:11

#1

'Cause God loved us
so much, he let his
boy be killed so that
those that believe in
him won't hang up
in the stirrup and
die, but will have
eternal life in heaven.

John 3:16

Alphabetical Index

Verse	Order
1 Corinthians 6:19	69
1 Corinthians 10:13	38
2 Corinthians 5:17	41
2 Corinthians 5:21	52
2 Corinthians 12:9	43
1 John 1:9	19
1 John 3:16	70
1 Peter 2:24	91
1 Peter 3:15	32
1 Peter 5:7	36
2 Peter 1:4	83

Verse	Order
2 Timothy 1:7	50
2 Timothy 3:16	33
Acts 1:8	49
Acts 2:38	59
Acts 4:12	89
Acts 17:11	66
Acts 18:9	16
Acts 18:10	15
Acts 18:11	17
Colossians 3:12	63
Colossians 3:23	94
Ephesians 2:10	37
Ephesians 2:8	11

Verse	Order
Ephesians 2:9	28
Ephesians 3:20	60
Galatians 2:20	18
Galatians 5:22	12
Galatians 5:23	30
Genesis 1:1	5
Genesis 1:26	46
Genesis 1:27	62
Hebrews 4:12	73
Hebrews 4:15	99
Hebrews 4:16	86
Hebrews 10:25	82
Hebrews 11:1	40

Verse	Order
Hebrews 11:6	55
Hebrews 12:1	64
Hebrews 12:2	35
Hebrews 13:5	42
Isaiah 26:3	90
Isaiah 40:31	27
Isaiah 41:10	45
Isaiah 53:4	51
Isaiah 53:5	31
Isaiah 53:6	58
Isaiah 55:8	98
James 1:2	57
James 1:3	79

Verse	Order
James 1:12	78
James 5:16	65
Jeremiah 29:11	2
John 1:1	68
John 1:12	77
John 3:16	1
John 3:17	88
John 5:24	56
John 10:10	14
John 11:25	54
John 13:35	100
John 14:27	72
John 14:6	21

Verse	Order
John 15:13	74
John 16:33	48
Joshua 1:8	92
Joshua 1:9	26
Matthew 5:16	97
Matthew 6:33	34
Matthew 11:28	39
Matthew 11:29	47
Matthew 11:30	61
Matthew 22:37	95
Matthew 28:18	93
Matthew 28:19	10
Matthew 28:20	22

Verse	Order
Micah 6:8	75
Philippians 1:6	84
Philippians 4:6	9
Philippians 4:7	25
Philippians 4:8	24
Philippians 4:13	4
Philippians 4:19	67
Proverbs 3:5	6
Proverbs 3:6	7
Psalm 37:4	87
Psalm 133:1	71
Psalm 133:2	96
Psalm 133:3	85

Verse	Order
Romans 3:23	20
Romans 5:8	23
Romans 6:23	29
Romans 8:28	3
Romans 8:38	80
Romans 8:39	81
Romans 10:9	44
Romans 10:17	76
Romans 12:1	13
Romans 12:2	8
Romans 15:13	53

Made in the USA
Columbia, SC
20 November 2018